A New Tune *for* Viola

The viola edition of *A New Tune A Day* is designed to be used seamlessly with the violin and cello editions. Teachers wishing to accommodate all instruments together in a lesson will be able to do so with almost every piece of every lesson, including the duets and rounds.

The few exceptions, in lessons 1, 2 and 7, are indicated as being for viola and cello only by the heading 'Viola Special':

look for this symbol within the book ✳

Boston Music Company
part of The Music Sales Group
London/New York/Paris/Sydney/Copenhagen/Berlin/Madrid/Tokyo

Foreword

Since its appearance in the early 1930s, C. Paul Herfurth's original *A Tune A Day* series has become the most popular instrumental teaching method of all time. Countless music students have been set on their path by the clear, familiar, proven material, and the logical, sensibly-paced progression through the lessons within the book.

The teacher will find that the new books have been meticulously rewritten by experienced teachers: instrumental techniques and practices have been updated and the musical content has been completely overhauled.

The student will find clearly-presented, uncluttered material, with familiar tunes and a gentle introduction to the theoretical aspects of music. The books are now accompanied by audio CDs of examples and backing tracks to help the student develop a sense of rhythm, intonation and performance at an early stage.

As in the original books, tests are given following every five lessons. Teachers are encouraged to present these as an opportunity to ensure that the student has a good overview of the information studied up to this point.

The following extract from the foreword to the original edition remains as true today as the day it was written:

The value of learning to count aloud from the very beginning cannot be over-estimated. Only in this way can a pupil sense rhythm.

Class teaching should be a combination of individual instruction and ensemble playing. At every lesson there should be individual playing so that all the necessary corrections can be made. Never allow pupils' mistakes to go unnoticed, since only by immediate correction will they develop the habit of careful thinking and playing.

Many teachers do the thinking for their pupils, instead of helping them to think for themselves. Insisting upon the mastery of each point will not dull their interest.

Music-making is a lifelong pleasure, and at its heart is a solid understanding of the principles of sound production and music theory. These books are designed to accompany the student on these crucial first steps: the rewards for study and practice are immediate and lasting. Welcome to the world of music!

Contents

Published by
Boston Music Company

Exclusive Distributors:
Music Sales Limited
8/9 Frith Street, London W1D 3JB, England.
Music Sales Corporation
257 Park Avenue South, New York, NY10010, USA.
Music Sales Pty Limited
120 Rothschild Avenue, Rosebery, NSW 2018, Australia.

This book © Copyright 2006 Boston Music Company,
a division of Music Sales Limited

Edited by David Harrison
Music processed by Paul Ewers Music Design
Original compositions and arrangements by Sarah Pope and Janet Coles
Cover and book designed by Chloë Alexander
Photography by Matthew Ward
Model: Ben Cartlidge
Printed in the EU
Backing tracks by Guy Dagul
CD performance by Catherine Bradshaw
CD recorded, mixed and mastered by Jonas Persson and John Rose

Your Guarantee of Quality
As publishers, we strive to produce every book to the highest commercial
standards. The music has been freshly engraved and the book has been
carefully designed to minimise awkward page turns and to make playing
from it a real pleasure. Throughout, the printing and binding have been
planned to ensure a sturdy, attractive publication which should give years
of enjoyment. If your copy fails to meet our high standards, please inform
us and we will gladly replace it.

www.musicsales.com

Rudiments of music

The stave

Music is written on a grid of five lines called a *stave*.
At the beginning of each stave is placed a special symbol called a *clef* to describe the approximate range of the instrument for which the music is written.

This example shows an *alto clef*, generally used for viola.

The stave is divided into equal sections of time, called *bars* or *measures*, by *barlines*.

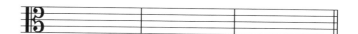

Note values

Different symbols are used to show the time value of *notes*, and each *note value* has an equivalent symbol for a rest, representing silence.

The **quaver** (or *eighth note*), often used to signify a half beat, is written with a solid head and a stem with a tail. The quaver rest is also shown.

The **crotchet** (or *quarter note*), often used to signify one beat, is written with a solid head and a stem. The crotchet rest is also shown.

The **minim** (or *half note*) is worth two crotchets. It is written with a hollow head and a stem. The minim rest is placed on the middle line.

The **semibreve** (or *whole note*) is worth two minims. It is written with a hollow head. The semibreve rest hangs from the fourth line.

Other note values

Note values can be increased by half by adding a dot after the note head. Here a minim and a crotchet are together worth a *dotted* minim.

Grouping quavers

Where two or more quavers follow each other, they can be joined by a *beam* from stem to stem.

Time signatures

The number of beats in a bar is determined by the *time signature*, a pair of numbers placed after the clef.
The upper number shows how many beats each bar contains, whilst the lower number indicates what kind of note value
is used to represent a single beat. This lower number is a fraction of a semibreve so that 4 represents crotchets
and 8 represents quavers.

𝄴, for *common time*, is
another way to write ⁴₄.

⁶₈ means six quavers to the bar.

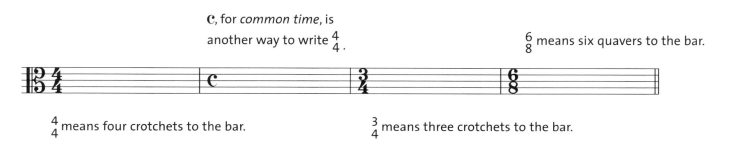

⁴₄ means four crotchets to the bar.

³₄ means three crotchets to the bar.

Note names

Notes are named after the first seven letters of the alphabet and are written on lines or spaces on the stave,
according to pitch.

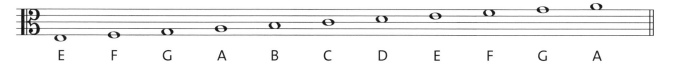

E   F   G   A   B   C   D   E   F   G   A

Accidentals

The pitch of a note can be altered up or down a half step (or *semitone*) by the use of sharp and flat symbols.
These temporary pitch changes are known as accidentals.

The *sharp* (♯) raises the pitch of a note.

The *natural* (♮) returns the note to its original pitch.

The *flat* (♭) lowers the pitch of a note.

Ledger lines

Ledger lines are used to extend the range of the stave for low or high notes.

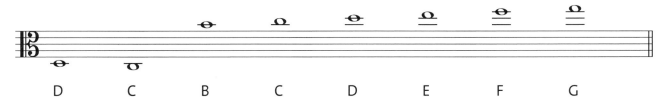

D   C   B   C   D   E   F   G

Bar lines

Various different types of bar lines are used:

Double bar lines divide one section of music from another.

Final bar lines show the end of a piece of music.

Repeat marks show a section to be repeated.

Before you play:

Accessories

Before your first viola lesson, make sure you have these items to go with your viola, bow and case:

• **Rosin** – derived from pine resin – to rub on to the bow hair before playing. It makes the hair sticky so that it grips the strings.

• **Duster** to remove rosin dust from the viola after playing.

• **Spare strings** are not interchangeable. They come in packets identified by letter names and numbers:

    A = I   D = II   G = III   C = IV

They are sold separately or in sets.

• **Chin rest** is usually attached to the viola when you buy it. Helps you hold the viola and protects it.
Can be bought separately if you need a different design.

• **Shoulder rest** to help you hold the viola. There are many designs available. Ask your teacher.

• **Music stand**. Make sure you adjust it for your eye level – standing or sitting – so it will help you to develop good posture when playing.

• **Tuning assistance**. Violas frequently need to be tuned. See opposite for instructions: use a keyboard, an electronic tuner, or the tuning tracks on the accompanying CD to help you find the right note, or ask your teacher to show you how to use a tuning fork.

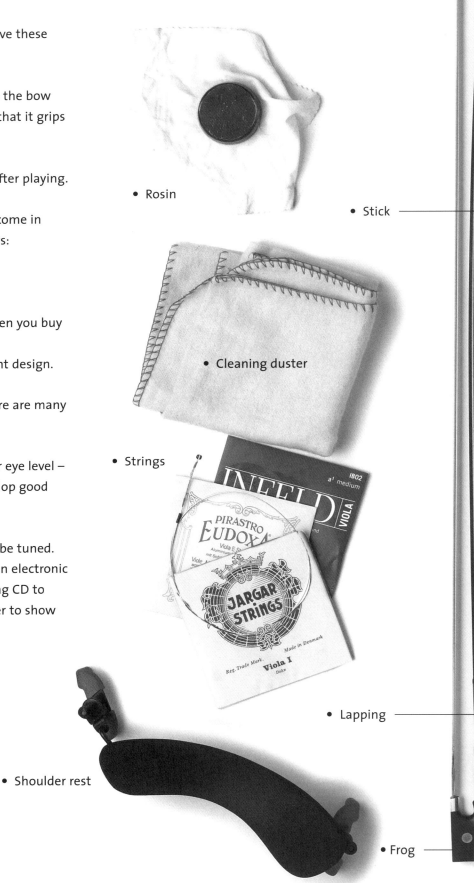

• Point

• Hair

• Rosin

• Stick

• Cleaning duster

• Strings

• Lapping

• Shoulder rest

• Frog

• Screw

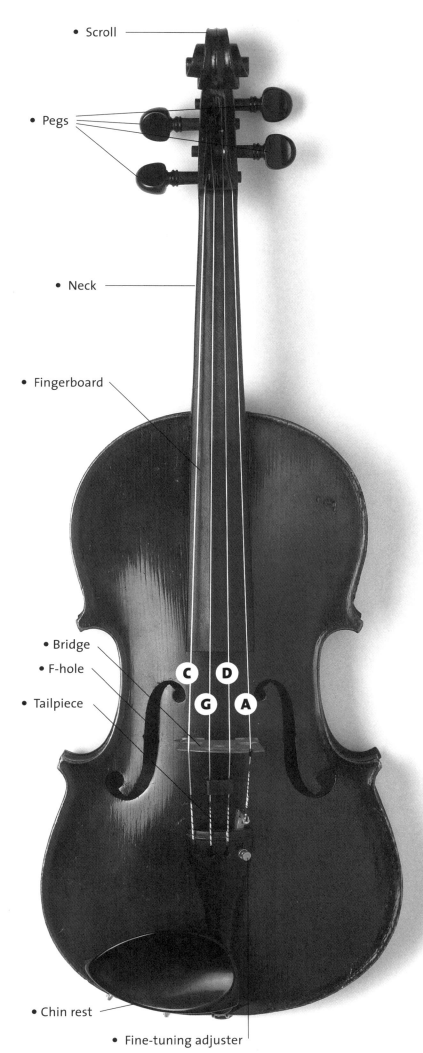

- Scroll
- Pegs
- Neck
- Fingerboard
- Bridge
- F-hole
- Tailpiece
- Chin rest
- Fine-tuning adjuster

C D
G A

Tuning

Your teacher will show you how to tune your viola using the pegs and the fine-tuning adjusters. If your viola does not have adjusters it is a good idea to have them fitted because they are easier to use than the pegs. There may be a reason why your viola should not have them though, so check with your teacher or viola shop.

The pegs can be difficult to manage at first and need some practice. If you have the choice of pegs and adjusters, only use the pegs if the strings are very out of tune. Never tune the strings higher than the required note with the pegs, or the strings are in danger of breaking. Tune to just below the note with the pegs then complete the fine tuning with the adjusters.

Most players tune the **A** string first as it is the common tuning note for orchestras and ensembles.

How to tune:

Sound a long A on your keyboard or accompanying CD.
Listen until you can sing or hum the A.
You may have to try this a few times.

Now play the A string (pluck or bow), and sing the note it produces. Decide whether it sounds the same as the keyboard/CD note.

If the string sounds too low ('flat'), tighten the tuning adjuster by turning it clockwise. If the string sounds too high ('sharp'), loosen the tuning adjuster by turning it anticlockwise.

New strings can go out of tune quite quickly until they have been stretched to their required pitch for a while and "settle down".

Take care when carrying your viola because knocks and bumps can make it go out of tune.

Before you play:

Care of the viola and bow

Your viola is made of wood – usually maple and pine –
so beware:

COLD, DRY or DAMP can:

• Make it go out of tune

• Make it warp and crack

So keep your viola at an even temperature:

Never store your viola beside a heater

Never store your viola in a hot or cold parked car

When you unpack your viola always take the bow out first.
and put it in last when you pack it up.

The bow

After playing, remember to loosen the tension of the bow
to allow the stick to maintain its shape and flexibility.

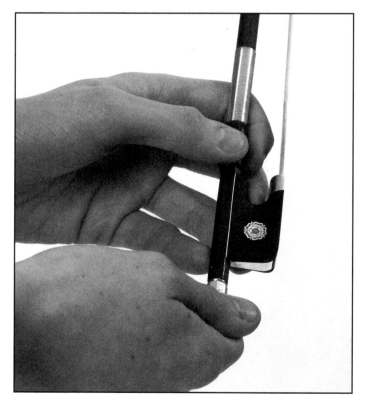

Avoid touching the bow hair – or the bow will lose its grip.

Cleaning

Use a duster without polish, chemical products or water.

The bridge and soundpost are held in place by the tension
of the strings. They are not glued in position (to allow for
adjustment). Never take all the strings off at once or the
bridge and soundpost may become displaced.

Posture

Standing to play the viola allows easier balance and more freedom of movement than sitting.

Place the viola (with shoulder rest if you are using one) on your left collarbone.

Keep your natural body alignment – look straight ahead.

Drop the head slightly until the left side of the jaw meets the chin rest and you can hold the viola without raising your shoulder.

With fingers curved and thumb relaxed, rest the viola neck against the left thumb to share the weight of the viola with your left shoulder.

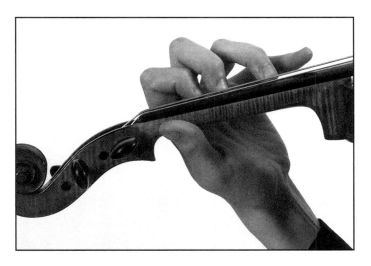

Avoid gripping the neck of the viola between finger and thumb.

Holding the bow

Make a circle with your 2nd finger overlapping the tip of the thumb.

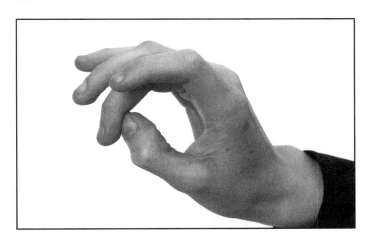

Place the bow between 2nd finger and thumb and let the neighbouring fingers curve round the stick. The little fingertip rests on top of the stick.

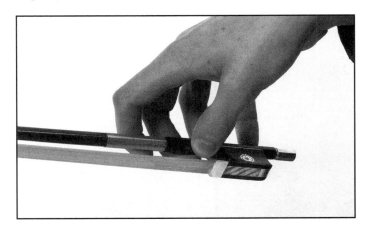

Lesson 1 goals:

1. **Name and play the open strings**
2. **Learn the value of minims and crotchets**

Part 1 – Viola Special: this section is not compatible with the violin book

Pizzicato

Pizzicato is a technique used to play without the bow

Plucking the string, known as *pizzicato*, is a technique used to perform on the viola without the bow.

Use your right hand first or second finger, resting your thumb against the fingerboard. Pull the string sideways with the fleshy part of the finger.

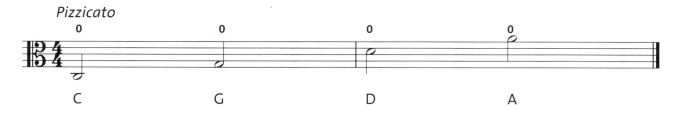

Pizzicato

C   G   D   A

Minims look like this: and are worth a count of **2**   **Crotchets** look like this: and are worth a count of **1**

Pizzicato

Count: 1   2   3   4   1   2   3   4

Before you begin, count a steady '1, 2, 3, 4' several times and keep counting while you play.

Pizzicato

C   C   G   G   D   D   A   A

Count: 1   2   3   4

6–7

Exercise 1:

Play this exercise through several times until your pizzicato strokes are nice and even.

Pizzicato

C   G   D   A

Count: 1   2   3   4

Sight-reading: Spell and play the following words

A   D   D
Play the word   Spell and play

 Part 2 – this section is compatible with the violin book

Tambour on the D string

1. Try singing the tune on the lower line with your teacher.

2. Clap your line and count aloud.

3. Join in while your teacher plays the tune.

Tambour on the A string

Sight-reading is an essential skill for a musician.

You'll be surprised how much easier this becomes with practice.

 8–9

The same piece is played here in two different keys: once in D and once in A. Notice how, in the first version, the melody on the second line of music seems to come happily to rest on the last note, D, whereas in the second example it's an A that brings the piece finally to a close.

Pieces for Lesson 1

Tambour verse 2 on the D and A strings

1. Try singing the tune on the lower line with your teacher.

2. Clap your line and count aloud.

3. Join in while your teacher plays the tune.

Hoe Down

1. Try singing the tune on the lower line with your teacher.

2. Clap your line and count aloud.

3. Join in while your teacher plays the tune.

The rest symbol − in the empty bars indicates a whole bar's rest.

goals:

1. **Down bows and up bows**
2. **Using fast bow strokes**
3. **Bowing on crotchets and minims**

*Part 1 – Viola Special: this section is **not** compatible with the violin book*

BOWING

⊓ *Down bow* means **pull** the bow to the **right**.

∨ *Up bow* means **push** the bow to the **left**.

Good posture will help you to retain a correct bowing technique.

In the following pieces you will find bowing signs ⊓ and ∨ to help you plan your bow strokes. Make sure you have enough bow for long or short notes: use a longer bow stroke for long notes such as minims and a shorter stroke for short notes such as crotchets.

Notice how bowing strokes alternate between ⊓ and ∨ .

Where no stroke is indicated, continue to alternate between up and down strokes.

Exercise 1:

In this piece, use quick alternating bow strokes. *Arco* means 'use the bow'.

12–13

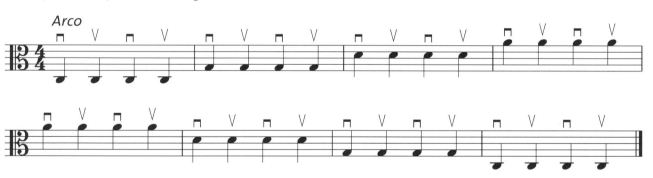

Exercise 2:

Now use a mixture of short and long bow strokes to fit the rhythm of the words.

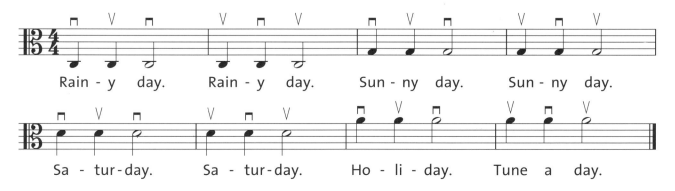

Lesson 2

Pieces for Lesson 2

 Part 2 – this section is compatible with the violin book

Tambour verse 1

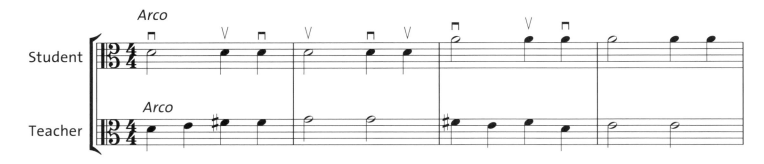

14-15 *Frère Jacques*

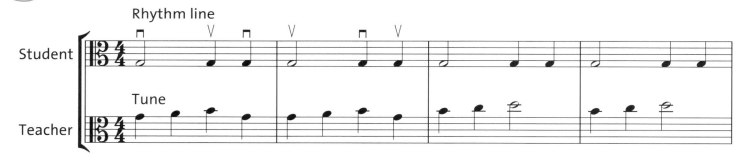

Now sing the tune of Frère Jacques.

Can you sing the tune and play the rhythm line on your viola at the same time?

Pieces for Lesson 2

Au Clair de la Lune

After the two bowing signs, continue with the alternating 'to & fro' actions for the rest of the piece.

Hoe Down

* (Viola Special)

Lesson 3 goals:

1. **Finger pattern one**
2. **Know the terms Pizzicato and Arco**
3. **Name and play the notes E, F♯ and G on the D string, and the note B on the A string**
4. **Recognise the sharp sign ♯**

The fingers of the left hand are numbered, from 1 to 4, according to the picture below.

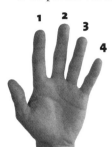

First finger on the D string

0 means play the string with no fingers on it (open), and **1** means use the first finger.

Sing the notes and then play *pizzicato*:

First finger on the A string

You will often find that viola music contains small numbers placed directly above the notes to indicate which finger should be used.

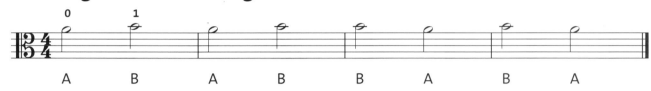

18–19 ## *Hoe Down*

Play this piece *pizzicato* at first, then try it *arco*:

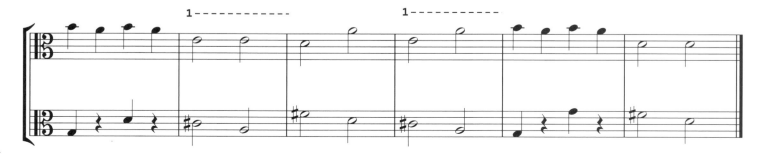

16

First, second and third fingers on the D string

Take a look at the pull-out fingering chart
to see where the sharps fall.

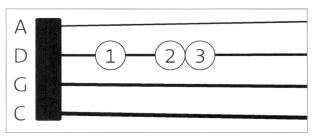

*Notice how much
smaller the gap
between the 2nd
and 3rd fingers is
than between the
1st and 2nd.*

*You will learn more
about this in lesson 4.*

Keep each finger down as you go higher.

When you reach G with the 3rd finger, listen to make sure that it's in tune with the open G string.

Sight-reading

Spell and play the following words. The ♯ isn't part of the word!

Tambour (verse 1)

Play this piece *pizzicato* at first, then try it *arco*:

Merrily We Roll Along

20-21

Again, try this piece *pizzicato* at first, then play it *arco*:

17

Lesson 4

goals:

1. **New notes on the A string: the D major scale**
2. **Crotchet rests and minim rests**
3. **Re-takes**
4. **The semibreve**
5. **Time signatures**

Notice how the basic finger positions for the A string are the same as for the D string.

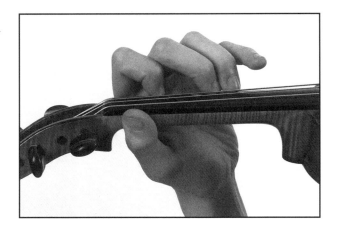

Notes on the A string

The finger pattern opposite show a whole tone gap between the 1st and 2nd fingers, and a semitone between the 2nd and 3rd – which are close together. The distance of a tone is twice as wide as a semitone

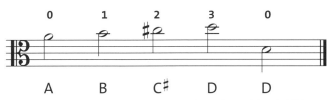

The major scale

The notes of the major scale follow a particular pattern of intervals.

Most of the notes are a tone apart, but between the 3rd and 4th notes of the scale, and again between the 7th and 8th notes of the scale, the interval is only half as much: a semitone.

Tone	Tone	Semitone	Tone	Tone	Tone	Semitone
1 2	3	4	5	6	7	8

D major scale

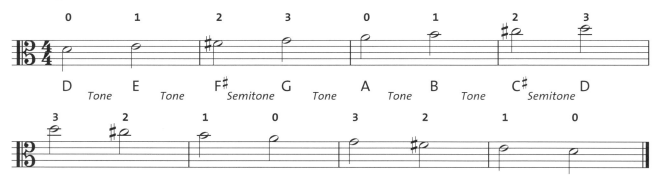

Is the high D on the A string in tune with the open D string?

Crotchet and minim rests

Rests are silences.

Crotchet rests are shown like this:

Minim rests are shown like this:

Exercise 1: hand shape

Practise this piece for a consistent left hand shape.

18

Pieces for Lesson 4

Au Clair de la Lune

'Re-take' means: lift the bow and prepare for the next bow stroke in the same direction

re-take here

Notice the note symbol in the last bar: it is a semibreve, worth four crotchets.

Whose Cuckoo? (a round)

When you reach the end of this piece, play it again from the beginning.

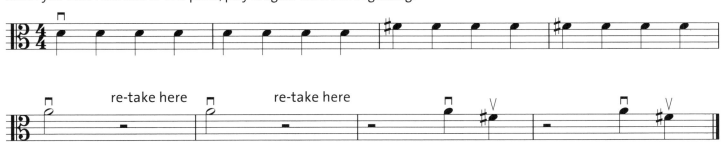

re-take here   re-take here

A new player can begin every two bars.

Take a look at the information on time signatures in the Rudiments of Music section (pages 4 and 5).

The following pieces use time signatures giving either four beats or three beats in each bar.

London Bridge Is Falling Down

Play this piece pizzicato at first, then try it arco:

French Folk Song

This piece has three beats to the bar. The top number in the time signature indicates the number of beats.

Lesson 5 goals:

1. **Quavers**
2. **Key signatures**
3. **Repeats**

The pieces in this lesson feature quavers, each worth half a crotchet.

They are written singly with flags, and can be joined together with **beams**:

Learn to recognise patterns of notes and the rhythms they make: it will make sight-reading so much easier.

1 & 2 &

Pease Pudding Hot

Clap the rhythm and count aloud, then continue to count as you play.

Count: 1 & 2 & 1 & 2 &

re-take here

The dots at the final barline are **repeat** markings: when you reach this sign go back to the beginning and play the piece for a second time.

26–27

Lavender's Blue

Key signatures

Often a piece of music contains some sharp signs at the beginning. This is the 'Key Signature'.

This sharp sign is on the F space of the stave. It means that all Fs in the music should be played as F♯.

This time there are sharp signs in the F space and on the C line: all the Fs will be F♯ and all the Cs will be C♯. This piece therefore uses the notes of the D major scale.

Pieces for Lesson 5

Frère Jacques (a round)

This piece has the key signature of D major.

A new player can begin every two bars.

Go From My Window

28-29

Kookaburra (a round)

re-take here

A new player can begin every two bars.

Supplementary Pieces

Ave Maria (a round for three players)

re-take

A new player can begin every two bars.

 30-31 *Old Oxford* (adapted)

Donkeys And Carrots (a round for four players)

Re-take bow

Re-take bow

Hee - Haw   Hee - Haw

A new player can begin every two bars.

 32-33 *Autumn* (from the *Four Seasons*)   Vivaldi

test: *for* Lessons 1 to 5

1. Missing words

Write the missing words in this sentence:

We went to the .... and .... ordered some

.... It was ....

(4)

2. Rests

On the stave below, draw rests of the indicated duration:

| A whole bar | 2 beats | 1 beat | 3 beats |

(4)

3. Notes

On the stave below draw the following notes as minims:

G, B, E, C, A, D and **F♯**

(7)

4. Find the sharp notes

How many of these notes are sharps? _____ Check the key signature.

(5)

5. Fingers

Write the correct finger numbers above the notes:

(5)

Total (25)

1. **Notes on the G string**
2. **Dynamics: loud and quiet**
3. **Repeats: first and second endings**
4. **Dotted minims**
5. **Whole bar's rest**
6. **Legato**

Notes on the G string

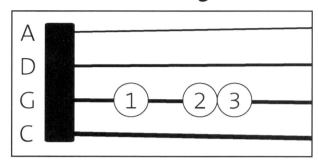

Notice how the fingers are placed in exactly the same way as for the D string and A string.

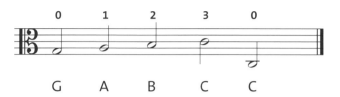

Dynamics

Music uses Italian words to describe how loudly or quietly to play.

These words or abbreviations are called 'Dynamic Markings'.

Forte (written as f) = **loud**

Piano (written as p) = **quiet**

Twinkle Twinkle Little Star

G major scale

Have a good look at the key signature and remember to play the correct sharps.

Try to sing the G major scale as you play it, and you'll find it has exactly the same 'melody' as the D major scale in lesson 4. It has the same sequence of tones and semitones.

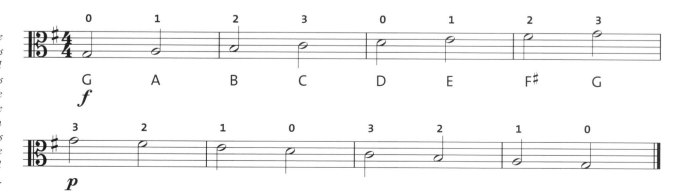

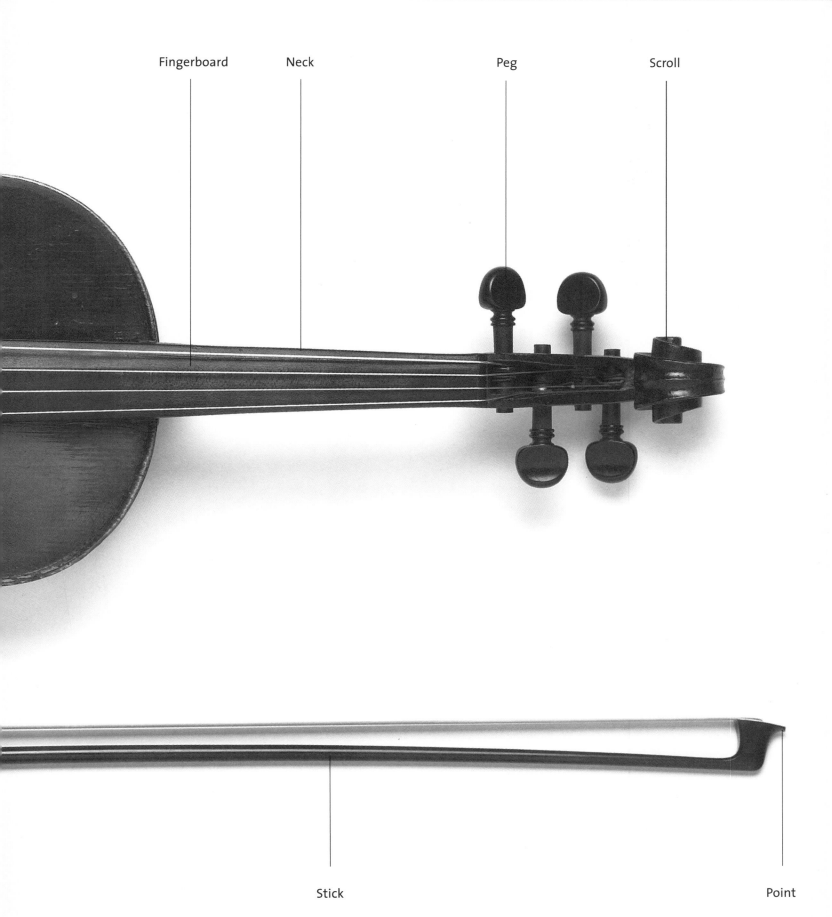

Fingerboard   Neck   Peg   Scroll

Stick   Point

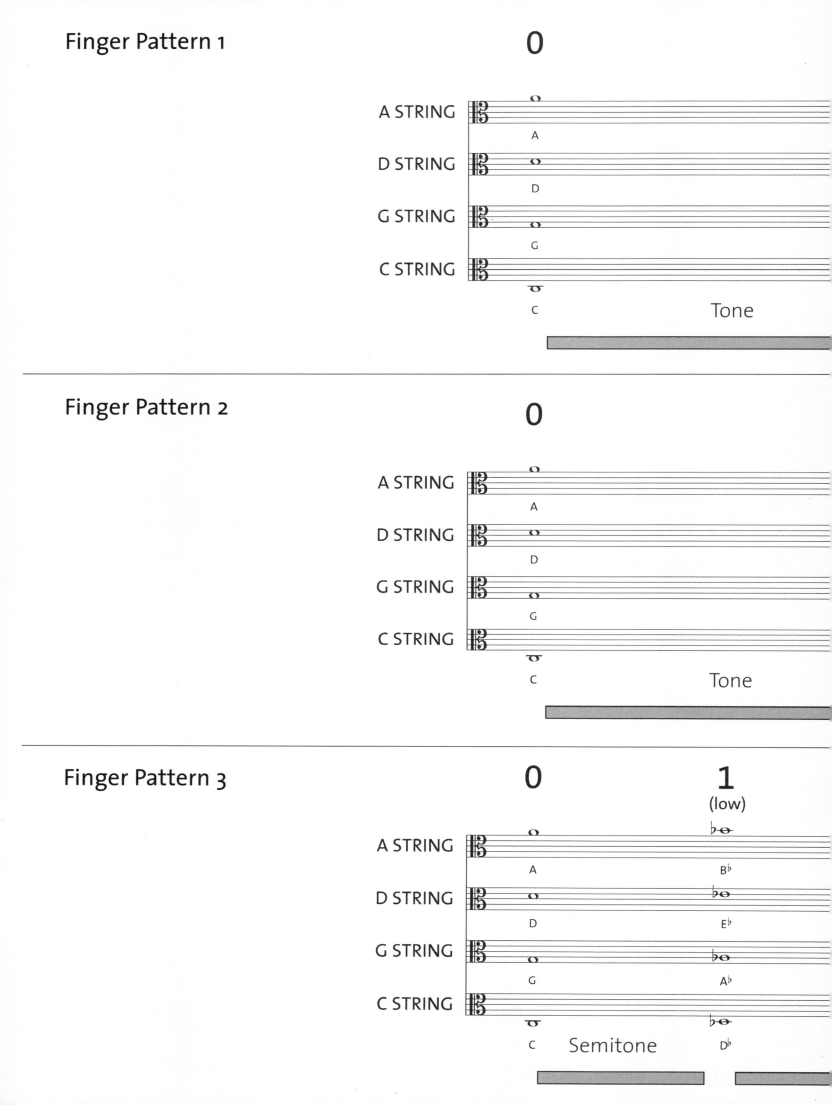

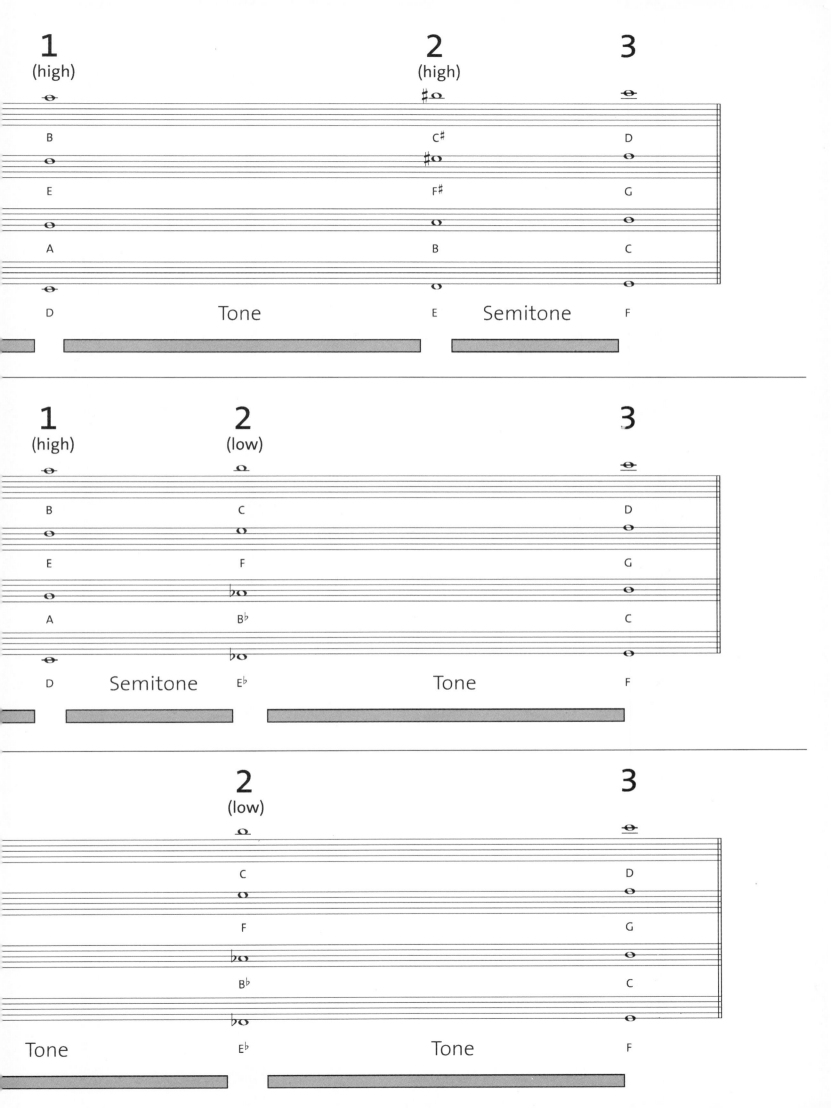

Chin rest   Tailpiece   Fine-tuning
                          adjuster   Bridge   F-hole

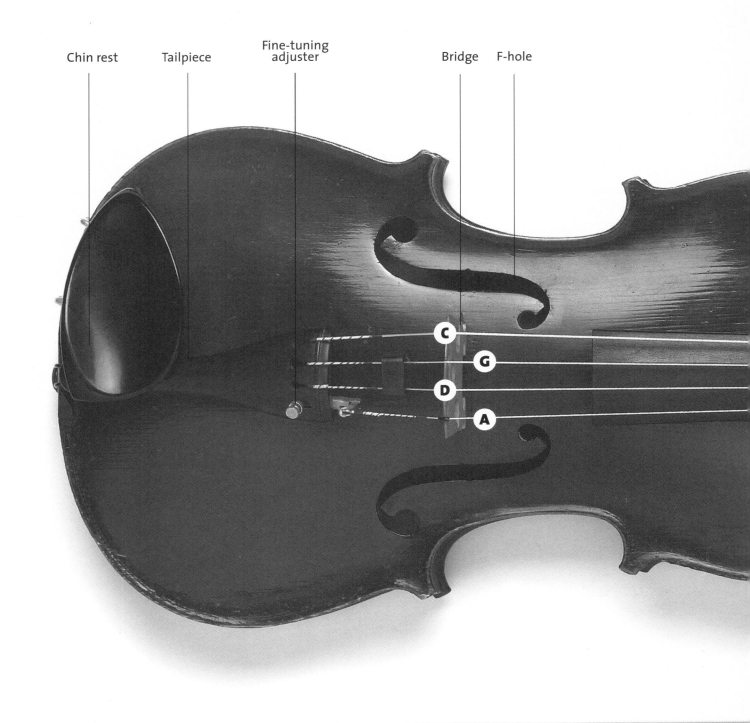

C
G
D
A

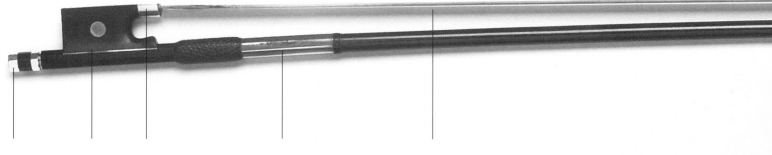

Screw   Frog   Ferrule   Lapping   Hair

Pieces for Lesson 6

First and second endings

In the following piece play to the repeat mark including the 1st time ending and repeat from the beginning.

On the second time through the piece miss out the 1st time ending and play the 2nd time ending instead.

Start with an up bow at the point. On the repeat this will be a down bow.

The Can Can
Offenbach **34–35**

1. *(1st time ending)*   2. *(2nd time ending)*

Ode To Joy (from *Symphony no.9*)
Beethoven **36–37**

legato means smoothly

Dotted minims

A dot beside a note adds half the length of the note: 𝅗𝅥. = 𝅗𝅥 + ♩

Largo (from the *New World Symphony*)
Dvořák

re-take bow

The rest symbol ▬ at the end of each line in this piece indicates a whole bar's rest.

Lesson 7 goals:

1. **Notes on the C string**
2. **Tied notes**
3. **Up beats**

 Viola Special: this lesson is not compatible with the violin book

Notes on the C string

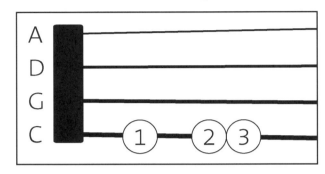

Here is the familiar finger pattern, this time for the C string.

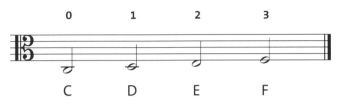

Tied notes

A note can be extended by tying it to another note of the same pitch.

This is shown by a curved line, joining two notes that make one continuous sound.

Keep the bow going smoothly in the same direction for the two tied notes.

Row, Row, Row Your Boat (a round for up to 4 players)

p

tie

Count: 1 2 3 1 2

re-take bow

A new player can begin every four bars.

C major scale (ascending and descending)

Check the key signature: no sharps (and no flats)

Pieces for Lesson 7

Country Garden

38 39

Czech Folk Song

Listen for the ringing sound when you play low D on the C string; If it is in tune the open D will 'ring' with it.

Can you hear the ring on the last note?

Up beats

Sometimes a piece of music doesn't begin with a whole bar. The next piece on this page begins with a single beat representing the last beat of a bar. This short bar at the beginning (called an **up beat** or **anacrusis**) should be balanced by another short bar at the end. The two short bars together add up to a whole bar.

Amazing Grace

40 41

Tie

Count: 1   2   3   1   2

This Old Man

27

1. Finger pattern 2
2. C major scale: second octave

3. G major finger pattern
4. New dynamics: *mp* and *mf*

The C major scale requires no sharps in the key signature. Notice how the Fs and Cs are natural: they are played a semitone lower than the F♯ and C♯ that you have played up until now. Compare the positions of Cs and Fs in the diagram above with the previous patterns.

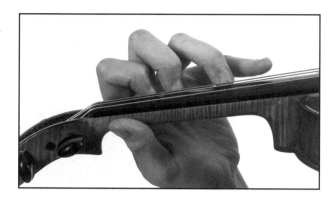

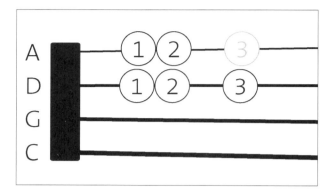

C major scale: second octave

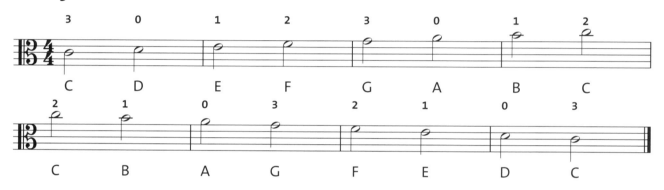

C D E F G A B C

C B A G F E D C

New dynamics

mp = mezzo piano, meaning moderately quiet (mezzo literally means 'half')

mf = mezzo forte, meaning moderately loud

42–43

Botany Bay

mp

mf

f

mp

G major finger pattern: second and third fingers

This exercise harmonises with the G major scale (second octave) in the violin book.

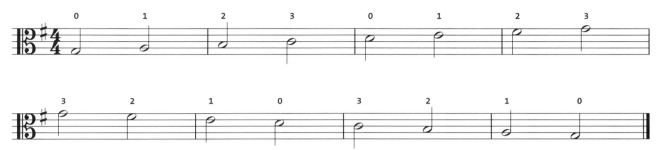

High 2nd or low 2nd?

Now you need to check your finger pattern: should you use your high or low 2nd finger?

A quick glance at the key signature will tell you which to use.

Pieces for Lesson 8

Andante (from the Surprise Symphony)

Haydn

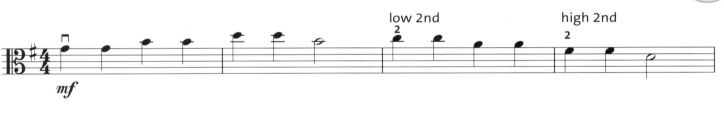

Grandfather's Clock

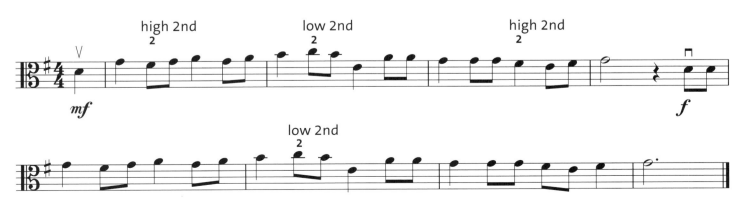

1. **Common time**
2. **Slurs**
3. **Crescendo and diminuendo**
4. **Dynamics:** *ff*

Common time

The $\frac{4}{4}$ time signature is often referred to as common time, and can be written like this: **C**

46-47

Jingle Bells

New dynamics

ff = fortissimo, meaning very loud

Hark! The Herald Angels Sing

*This piece is marked **mf** at the beginning. Don't start too loudly or you won't be able to build to a proper fortissimo by the end.*

Slurs

Slurring – playing two or more notes with the same bow direction – is an important bowing technique.
Slur symbols look just like ties, but they join two or more notes of different pitches.

Slurs across strings

Unto Us A Child Is Born

48-49

We Three Kings

Now practise slurring three notes to a single bow.

Music can gradually become louder or quieter, and the following Italian words are used to show this:

Crescendo – gradually louder   *Diminuendo* – gradually quieter

Good King Wenceslas

50-51

f

p   *crescendo*   *ff*

Start growing louder from the *p* marking until the *ff*:

31

Lesson 10 goals:

1. **Dotted crotchet**
2. **Dynamics: pianissimo**
3. **Crescendo and diminuendo 'hairpin' symbols**
4. **Repeated sections**

Dotted crotchet rhythm

A dot beside a crotchet adds half the length of the note: ♩. = ♩ + ♪

Exercise 1:

First, clap and count each of the following 3 lines, then play and count them.

Lines (b) and (c) should sound the same.

Notice how the same rhythm can be written in different ways. Get used to seeing patterns rather than reading each individual note.

Your performance will flow better and your sight-reading will improve.

Silent Night

Gruber

Remember: the 2nd beat starts on the 'dot' of the first crotchet.

Hairpins

Crescendo and diminuendo passages are often indicated by long 'hairpins' placed horizontally beneath the music.

52-53

While Shepherds Watched Their Flocks

This hairpin means *crescendo*

This hairpin means *diminuendo*

Pieces for Lesson 10

Deck The Halls

Count: 1 + 2 + 3 + 4 +

The First Noël

54-55

Notice that, since the repeated section doesn't start at the beginning of the piece, a separate repeat mark is needed for each end of the repeated section.

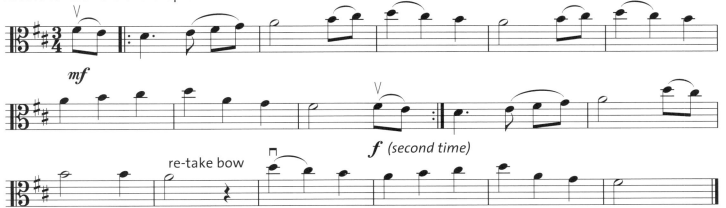

mf

f (second time)

re-take bow

New dynamics   *pp* = *pianissimo* meaning very quiet

Silent Night

56-57

pp legato

p

We Wish You A Merry Christmas

f   *ff*

Supplementary Pieces

58-59 *We Three Kings*

60-61 *Once In Royal David's City*

62-63 *Deck The Halls*

64-65 *Skaters' Waltz*

Waldteufel

test: *for* Lessons 6 to 10

1. Note duration

On the stave below, draw notes of the indicated duration:

I quaver	2 beats-worth of quavers	dotted crotchet	a note that lasts for 5 quavers

(8)

2. Scale

On the stave below, draw the G major scale including the correct key signature:

(4)

3. Notes

On the stave below draw the following notes as crotchets:

F, A, B, C♯, F♯, D, G and **E**

(4)

4. Dynamics

What are the Italian words for:

Moderately loud _____

Moderately quiet _____

(4)

5. Naming ceremony

What do these Italian words mean?   What do these signs mean?

legato   *pp*

arco   *mf*

crescendo   **c**

pizzicato   ◁

diminuendo   :‖

(5)

Total (25)

35

goals:

1. **Spiccato-lifted bow strokes**
2. **Tempo markings**

Spiccato

Try to visualise the bow movement as a little smile, beginning with the approach to the string and ending as the bow lifts off again.

This needs to be controlled and consistent.

Spiccato is a short, lifted bow stroke used to produce a detached (*staccato*) note.

Find a place in the lower half of the bow that gives you maximum control, and draw a smile with your bow as you lift it off the string.

Spiccato notes are marked like this:

Oats And Beans

Find the best part of the bow to control the landing and lifting.

mf

Did you find the best part of the bow?

Italian terms are often used to indicate the speed (tempo) of a piece:

Andante – at walking pace

Moderato – moderately

Allegretto – fairly quickly

Allegro – quickly

Andante (from the Surprise Symphony)

Haydn

p

Did you remember to lift the bow off the string?

Pieces for Lesson 11

Moderato (from the Peasant's Cantata)

Bach

mf

lift bow to finish

Did you remember to lift the bow off the string?

When you make spiccato bow strokes cushion your landings with flexible fingers and wrist.

London's Burning (a round)

f

A new player can begin every two bars.

Reuben And Rachel (a round for two players)

Allegretto

mf

f

re-take for repeat

A new player can begin after one bar.

Yankee Doodle

Allegro

f

Lesson 12

goals:

1. **Hooked bowings (broken slurs)**
2. **Quaver rests**
3. **Pause sign**
4. **Ritenuto**

Hooked bowing

Hooked bowing means playing two or more detached notes in the same bow direction.

It is usually written with a slur between two notes and lines on the note-heads, as in the example below.

Exercise 1:

Stop the bow after each note

This sign ⌢ is called a **pause** (or *fermata*). When this sign appears, the note should be held for longer than usual. The pause sign is sometimes found at the end of a piece of music.

70-71 *Scarborough Fair*

Moderato

mf

72-73 *Skye Boat Song*

Allegretto

re-take bow

p *legato*

re-take bow

mf

(2nd time)

p

Pieces for Lesson 12

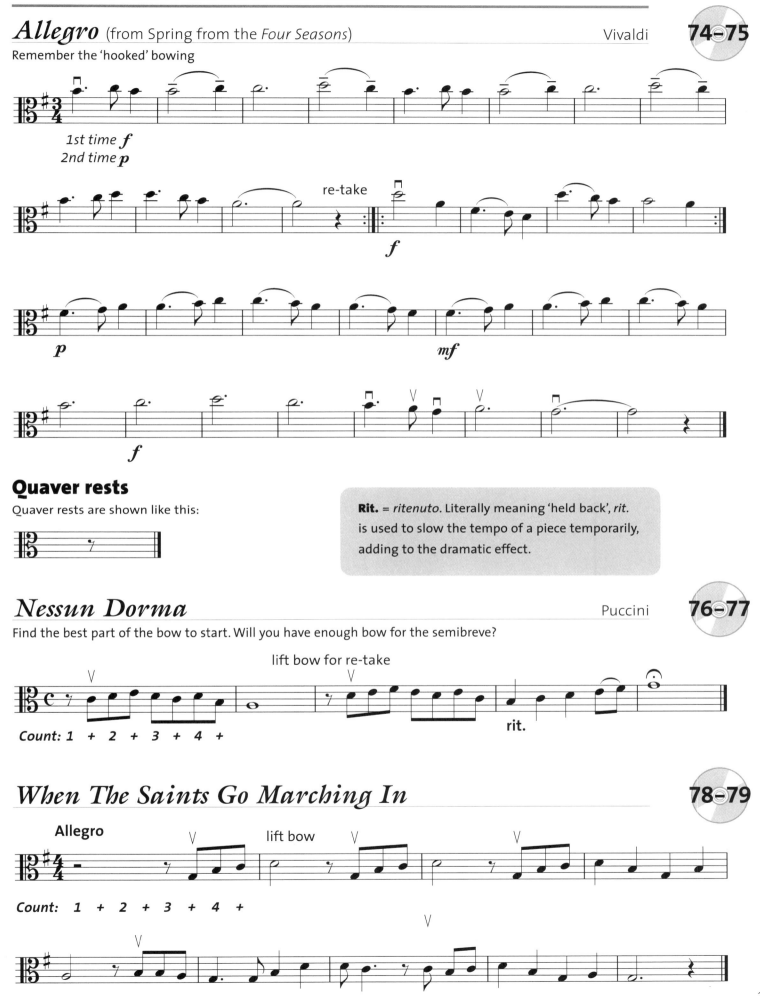

Allegro (from Spring from the *Four Seasons*)   Vivaldi   **74–75**

Remember the 'hooked' bowing

1st time *f*
2nd time *p*

re-take

f

p   *mf*

f

Quaver rests

Quaver rests are shown like this:

Rit. = *ritenuto*. Literally meaning 'held back', *rit.* is used to slow the tempo of a piece temporarily, adding to the dramatic effect.

Nessun Dorma   Puccini   **76–77**

Find the best part of the bow to start. Will you have enough bow for the semibreve?

lift bow for re-take

rit.

Count: 1 + 2 + 3 + 4 +

When The Saints Go Marching In   **78–79**

Allegro   lift bow

Count: 1 + 2 + 3 + 4 +

39

1. **Arpeggios**
2. **Composing a round**

Arpeggios

Have a look at the pieces of music in this book, and you'll discover that melodies are generally made from a combination of fragments of arpeggios and scale passages.

Arpeggios are made by playing the 1st, 3rd and 5th notes of a scale in sequence.

Many melodies have sections containing arpeggios. Scales and arpeggios should be practised regularly.

D major scale

Notice how Roman numerals are used to show the degree of the scale, and that the eighth note – the octave – is numbered the same as the first note.

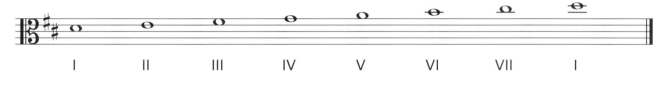

Practise both scales and arpeggios regularly, and you'll find it much easier to tackle new pieces of music.

D major arpeggio

The major arpeggio sounds like the first four notes of 'Morning Has Broken', reproduced opposite in G as the original Gaelic melody 'Bunessan'.

Sing this arpeggio first, then play it:

Now use the same finger pattern to play arpeggios starting on the G or C strings.

Fanfare (a round)

A new player can begin every half bar.

Now try making your own round using notes from an arpeggio of your choice.

Choose a rhythm pattern with 2, 3, or 4 beats to the bar, and write in the time signature.

Pieces for Lesson 13

Kumbayah

Notice how, in the second line, a new time signature is introduced for a single bar.

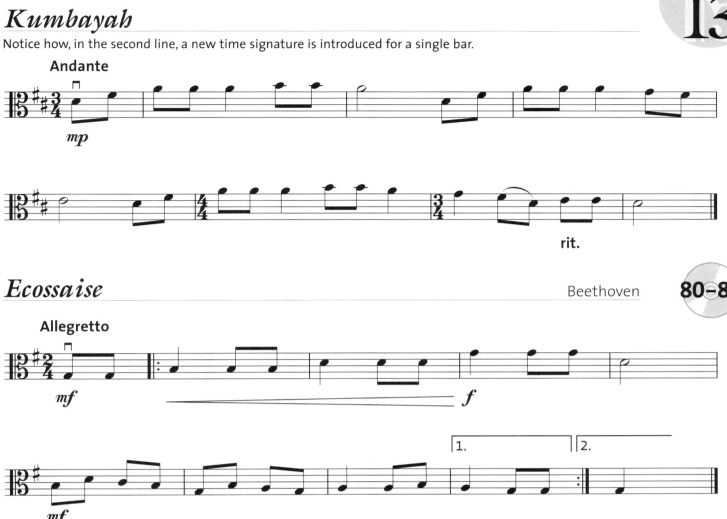

Ecossaise

Beethoven

Bunessan (Gaelic melody)

Lesson 14 goals:

1. **F major scale and arpeggio**
2. **New note B♭ on the G string**

You have learnt to play sharps in previous lessons and now you'll be looking at flats. How many different keys have you studied in this book? How would you go about playing some of the pieces in a different key?

The flat sign (♭) to the left of a note-head lowers the note by a semitone.

In the following scale the B is played as a B♭ to play the major scale: **T - T - S - T - T - T - S**

F major scale

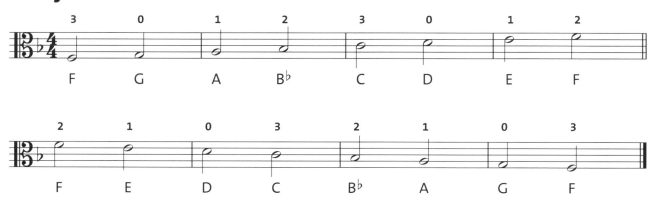

F G A B♭ C D E F

F E D C B♭ A G F

F major arpeggio

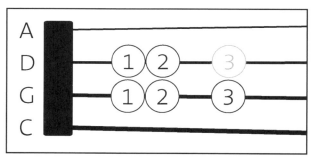

THINK!

When you play notes an octave apart (such as the first and last notes of a scale) do they really sound the same?

Octaves are an excellent way of checking your tuning, either against an open string or with both notes fingered.

42

Pieces for Lesson 14

Filou

Praetorius

In this piece the 2nd finger is required for the Bb.

Allegro

Abide With Me

Monk

84-85

Remember: 2nd finger Bb.

Andante

mp

crescendo

mf

The Happy Farmer

Schumann

Allegro

f

Lullaby

Brahms

86-87

Andante

pp

low 2nd finger

further techniques:

Tremolo

This is a technique using very quick bowing to create a shimmering sound.

It is indicated in music with lines over note stems like this:

Play *tremolo* with very fast little bow strokes near the point of the bow.

88-89 ### *Gymnopédie No. 1*

Satie

Mysteriously

tremolo here

90 ### *Skye Boat Song*

In this piece, play both the D and A strings all the time.

Playing notes on two strings together is known as *double stopping*.

Harmonics

Try sliding your left hand all the way up the D string and then back down, touching the string very lightly with your 3rd finger as you go. Bow near the bridge as you slide the finger and you will hear some strange ethereal sounds. These are the notes of the harmonic series.

Place your 4th finger very lightly on the D string halfway to the bridge, keeping your thumb at the base of the neck.

Play with a fast bowstroke near the bridge you will hear a flute-like ringing note one octave above the open D string: the octave harmonic.

Try sliding up to the octave harmonic as shown below.

Harmonics are indicated by a little circle over the note-head.

Try this technique on all your strings.

44

Pieces for Lesson 15

Lovely Evening (a round for three players)

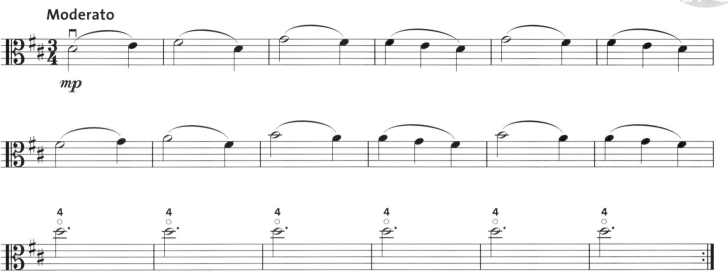

A new player can begin every six bars.

Sumer Is Icumen In (a round)

91

Slide the hand now

A new player can begin every four bars.

Seagulls

Slide your left hand all the way to the top
of the A string.

Now press the string down with your 3rd finger
and slide it away from the bridge fast, lots of times,
for about two centimetres.

Use a fast down bow for each slide, re-taking after
each stroke. You will sound like a flock of seagulls!

45

Supplementary Pieces

92-93

Theme (from First Symphony)

Brahms

Allegro

f *mp* *mf* *cresc.* *f* *rit.*

Canon (for up to 8)

Tallis

Moderato

mf

A new player can begin every four beats.

94-95

Auld Lang Syne

Moderato

mf *f* *rit.*

46

test: *for* Lessons 11 to 15

1. Key signatures

On the stave below, draw the correct key signatures for:

G major   F major   A minor   D major   C major

(5)

2. Dots

Simplify the music on the left using dots to get rid of the ties

(5)

3. Arpeggios

a: Put a ring round the notes that make an arpeggio

b: Which scale is this?

I   II   III   IV   V   VI   VII   I

(6)

4. Terms

What do the following terms mean:

Allegretto _____   Fermata _____

Spiccato _____   Ritenuto _____

(4)

5. Naming ceremony

Identify all the items indicated by arrows.

(5)

Total **(25)**

CD backing tracks

1   Tuning Note A
2   Tuning Note D
3   Tuning Note G
4   Tuning Note C
5   Virtuoso Performance
6   Lesson 1 Exercise 1 *Demonstration*
7   Lesson 1 Exercise 1 *Backing Only*
8   Tambour on the D string *Demonstration*
9   Tambour on the D string *Backing Only*
10 Hoe Down *Demonstration*
11 Hoe Down *Backing Only*
12 Lesson 2 Exercise 1 *Demonstration*
13 Lesson 2 Exercise 1 *Backing Only*
14 Frère Jacques *Demonstration*
15 Frère Jacques *Backing Only*
16 Au Clair de la Lune *Demonstration*
17 Au Clair de la Lune *Backing Only*
18 Hoe Down *Demonstration*
19 Hoe Down *Backing Only*
20 Merrily We Roll Along *Demonstration*
21 Merrily We Roll Along *Backing Only*
22 London Bridge Is Falling Down *Demonstration*
23 London Bridge Is Falling Down *Backing Only*
24 French Folk Song *Demonstration*
25 French Folk Song *Backing Only*
26 Lavender's Blue *Demonstration*
27 Lavender's Blue *Backing Only*
28 Go From My Window *Demonstration*
29 Go From My Window *Backing Only*
30 Old Oxford *Demonstration*
31 Old Oxford *Backing Only*
32 Autumn *Demonstration*
33 Autumn *Backing Only*
34 The Can Can *Demonstration*

35 The Can Can *Backing Only*
36 Ode To Joy *Demonstration*
37 Ode To Joy *Backing Only*
38 Country Garden *Demonstration*
39 Country Garden *Backing Only*
40 Amazing Grace *Demonstration*
41 Amazing Grace *Backing Only*
42 Botany Bay *Demonstration*
43 Botany Bay *Backing Only*
44 Andante *Demonstration*
45 Andante *Backing Only*
46 Jingle Bells *Demonstration*
47 Jingle Bells *Backing Only*
48 Unto Us A Child Is Born *Demonstration*
49 Unto Us A Child Is Born *Backing Only*
50 Good King Wenceslas *Demonstration*
51 Good King Wenceslas *Backing Only*
52 While Shepherds Watched Their Flocks *Demonstration*
53 While Shepherds Watched Their Flocks *Backing Only*
54 The First Noël *Demonstration*
55 The First Noël *Backing Only*
56 Silent Night *Demonstration*
57 Silent Night *Backing Only*
58 We Three Kings *Demonstration*
59 We Three Kings *Backing Only*
60 Once In Royal David's City *Demonstration*
61 Once In Royal David's City *Backing Only*
62 Deck The Halls *Demonstration*
63 Deck The Halls *Backing Only*
64 Skaters' Waltz *Demonstration*
65 Skaters' Waltz *Backing Only*
66 Moderato *Demonstration*
67 Moderato *Backing Only*
68 Yankee Doodle *Demonstration*
69 Yankee Doodle *Backing Only*
70 Scarborough Fair *Demonstration*
71 Scarborough Fair *Backing Only*

72 Skye Boat Song *Demonstration*
73 Skye Boat Song *Backing Only*
74 Allegro *Demonstration*
75 Allegro *Backing Only*
76 Nessun Dorma *Demonstration*
77 Nessun Dorma *Backing Only*
78 When The Saints Go Marching In *Demonstration*
79 When The Saints Go Marching In *Backing Only*
80 Ecossaise *Demonstration*
81 Ecossaise *Backing Only*
82 Bunessan *Demonstration*
83 Bunessan *Backing Only*
84 Abide With Me *Demonstration*
85 Abide With Me *Backing Only*
86 Lullaby *Demonstration*
87 Lullaby *Backing Only*
88 Gymnopédie No1 *Demonstration*
89 Gymnopédie No1 *Backing Only*
90 Skye Boat Song *Demonstration*
91 Sumer Is Icumen In *Demonstration*
92 Theme from First Symphony (Brahms) *Demonstration*
93 Theme from First Symphony (Brahms) *Backing Only*
94 Auld Lang Syne *Demonstration*
95 Auld Lang Syne *Backing Only*

How to use the CD

The tuning notes on tracks 1 to 4 are the notes of the open strings on the viola, beginning with the lowest string. After track 5, which gives an idea of how the viola can sound, the backing tracks are listed in the order in which they appear in the book. Look for the ⊙ symbol in the book for the relevant backing track. Where both parts of a duet are included on the CD, the top part is in the left channel, and the bottom part is in the right channel.

1 2 3 4 5 6 7 8 9